Illustrated by Bertina Dore'

Life as a tree.

My name is Woody,
and I am a tree.

I started out as a seed and planted in the ground to grow.

I grow roots below the ground.

I sprout out branches' and leaves.

I grow with the help of rain water and plenty of sunlight.

100 ft

50 ft

10 ft

1 ft

I can grow very tall; up to 100 feet high.

Leaves come in different colors and sizes.

My branches grow in different directions, and home to many animals.

Monkeys like to swing and play from my branches.

My branches hold a swing
for children to play.

I provide shade on hot and sunny days.

I grow acorns for the squirrels.

Trees like me grow many fruits like oranges, apples, and bananas.

Trees grow flowers for insects to eat.

My leaf pores gives oxygen
for clean air.

I give clean soil to grow flowers.

I can control noise.

Trees can be planted
anywhere.

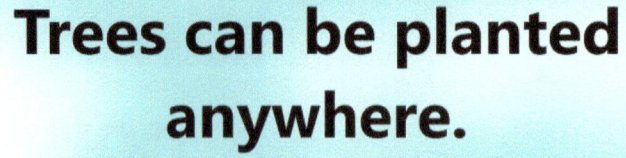

I live in a forest with all my family.

Trees help grow and nourish our families, animals, insects and our planet earth.

Arbor Day is celebrated annually on different dates depending on the climate and seasons. Help give back to our planet and animals. Plant a tree today.

So let's plant a tree today!

Woody

www.ingramcontent.com/pod-product-compliance
Lightning Source LLC
Chambersburg PA
CBHW060818290526
45792CB00005BB/1702